This publication is designed to provide accurate and the subject matter covered. It is sold with the unde engaged in rendering legal, accounting, or other pro other expert assistance is required, the services of a competent professional person should be sought.

© 2011 by Karyn L. Beach

Published by Lose the Excuses

(704) 719-3739
info@losetheexcusesnow.com
http://www.losetheexcusesnow.com

All rights reserved. The text of this publication, or any part thereof, may not be reproduced in any manner whatsoever without permission in writing from the publisher.

Printed in the United States of America.

10 9 8 7 6 5 4 3 2

Table of Contents

Introduction 1
3 Rules for Getting It Together 1
Getting Everyone Onboard 2
Pre-work 2
Working the Workbook 2

Week One 5

    Introduction 7
    Weekend Accelerators 7
    Extra 7
    Day 1: Refrigerator Run-Through 9
    Day 2: Cabinet Dive and Dump 9
    Day 3: Sort and Separate 10
    Day 4: Over and Under 10
    Day 5: Tupperware Test 11
    Keeping It Together (KIT) 12
    Weekend Accelerators 12
    Prep for Week Two 13

Week Two 15

    Introduction 17
    Weekend Accelerators 17
    Extra 17
    Day 8: Junk or Bunk? 19
    Day 9: Is It Good For You? 19
    Day 10: Toss the Gloss 19
    Day 11: All Together Now 20
    Day 12: The Same Thing All Over Again 21
    Keeping It Together (KIT) 21
    Weekend Accelerators 22
    Prep for Week Three 22

Week Three 25

    Introduction 27
    Weekend Accelerators 27
    Extra 28

Day 15: The Nightstand's Last Stand 29
Day 16: The Closet Flash 29
Day 17: The Dresser Dash 30
Day 18: The Dresser Top 30
Day 19: Shoes Blues (and Accessories too!) 31
Keeping It Together (KIT) 32
Weekend Accelerators 32
Prep for Week Four 33

Week Four 35

Introduction 37
Weekend Accelerators 37
Day 22: Put It in Its Place 38
Day 23: Mabel! Mabel! Get Those Papers Off the Table! 38
Day 24: Desk Is a Mess 39
Day 25: Filing Focus 39
Day 26: Lady's Choice 40
Keeping It Together (KIT) 40
Weekend Accelerators 41
And There You Have It! 41

Extra Stuff 43

List of Tasks 45
Contract 47
About Get It Together Girl Creator Karyn L. Beach 49

Foreword – The Focused 15

How do you eat an elephant?

One bite at a time.

Whether you are getting an education, losing weight or running a marathon, none of it happens overnight. You attend classes regularly and study a little bit every day. You change your eating habits a meal at a time. You run and increase the distance a little bit at a time. It's the small but consistent changes that make the biggest differences.

This workbook is a testament to the fact that small changes can yield big results. Just 15 minutes a day can get you organized. It can work for you; but only IF YOU WORK IT. Commit to devoting a quarter of an hour, five days a week and you will see the difference.

I truly believe in the power of the Focused 15. Once it works for you here, try it in other areas. Spend 15 minutes a day - walking, talking to your partner or your kids, in prayer and meditation, and if you do it consistently, you will see a difference.

The Focused 15 is also a great antidote to procrastination. You can do just about anything for 15 minutes. Take a task you are dreading (returning a few phone calls, filing, vacuuming) and give it 15 full, focused minutes. Again, you will be surprised at the progress you make. More often than not, you'll find whatever the task was, it wasn't so bad.

I'm excited that you took the time to invest in this program and I'm looking forward to the success you'll have with the Focused 15.

Now, go ahead and ... *Get It Together Girl!*

Introduction

When I say "get organized," you might have visions of impeccably color-coordinated closets and immaculate kitchens filled with alphabetized canned goods and fresh fruits organized by season. Maybe you see gleaming marble counter tops and bookshelves in subject then alphabetical order.

This is not that program!

I won't promise you perfection at the end of 28 days; but I can say, if you follow this program, you will:
- Cut the amount of time it takes to perform your daily chores.
- Spend less time looking for lost items.
- Develop easy routines and simple systems to keep you organized.

Organizing the *Get It Together Girl!* way will not take tons of time nor will it require you to break the bank. The only requirement is that you agree to spend 15 *focused* minutes a day, five days a week on the task at hand.

When it comes to weekends, you can take them off, or you can select one of the various Weekend Accelerators which will help you get organized faster.

You can complete the entire program in one month. If, as you go along, you find that some areas deserve more attention, you can revisit those areas later.

The program focuses on the following areas:
- Kitchen
- Bathroom
- Bedroom (and Closets)
- Office/Desk
- Living Room

As you get it together (GIT), I will give you tips on how to keep it together (KIT). The best part is that the KITs don't take 15 minutes. Most don't even take five. Many take a minute or less!

3 Rules for Getting It Together

1. **Spend 15 *Focused* Minutes.** This means 15 minutes where you are focused exclusively on the task at hand. You aren't watching television or going back and forth looking at emails. You are focused for 15 minutes, a quarter of an hour, exclusively on this one task.

2. **Time it**. You have a kitchen timer. Some are built right into the oven or microwave. You might have a timer feature on your cell phone. Use it. I am asking you to do 15 minutes, no more. Of course, if you get to the end of the 15 minutes and you've got

the momentum and the time to continue, feel free to keep going. But know that you don't *have to.*

3. **Make it Fun**. Play your favorite music while completing your assignment. Plan a weekend reward for each week of the program you complete successfully. Challenge yourself to see how much you can do. Agree on something fun to do with the family, or for yourself.

Getting Everyone Onboard

These tasks don't take a lot of time or effort. So get the husband/boyfriend/significant other/roommate involved. If you have a kid over the age of six, get them involved too.

Explain that you are getting organized in 15 minutes a day. Ask them to help you keep things organized by performing a task or two that will usually take less than a minute, and no more than five.

As a trainer who works with adult learners, I've learned a very important concept that works well when getting buy-in from family members. It's called *What's in It for Me.* Think about how this program will help each member of your family. Maybe Hubs would appreciate not having to look for his keys every morning. Your teen queen might like to learn a few ways to make cleaning her room and performing her chores a little easier and faster. Give them a reason, benefit, or reward that will appeal to them for following this plan with you.

Pre-work

If you don't know where to find them already, do a few Google searches and find your local food bank, Goodwill, Salvation Army and/or women's shelter. As you get rid of unwanted items, you might consider donating them to one of these groups.

Find a designated area for the items you need to get rid of. It can be in a basement, crawl space, garage, or closet, but you'll want a place where you can temporarily store the items you don't need but won't be throwing away immediately.

Once you've got the family on board, ask them what they want to do with unwanted/unneeded items: donations, garage sale, share with family members? Make this a fun family project.

Working the Workbook

Every weekday, there is a GIT (Get It Together) task. At the end of the week, you will find a list of KIT (Keep It Together) tips as well as potential Weekend Accelerators. You'll also be given a quick preview of the next week's activities.

Occasionally, you will see the following symbols:

Tip – something that you need to know

 Key – something that will make the assignment a little easier

 Thought – something to think about as you complete the task

At the end of the workbook, you will find a checklist of daily assignments. Check them off as you complete them. Post it on the refrigerator or in another visible area so you can see and track your progress. There is also a section for notes. Write any observations or jot down things you would like to come back and complete later, if 15 minutes is not enough.

Finally, there is a contract in the back. More than anything, this is a contract with yourself where you commit to completing the 28-day program. It is not legally binding. Rest assured, I won't track you down and haul you to court if you don't complete the program! However, I do want you to commit to it. This doesn't need to be a top priority, but it should be a priority. You will be pleasantly surprised at what you'll be able to accomplish in with such a small daily commitment.

Week One

"If you can organize your kitchen, you can organize your life."
~ Louis Parrish (author of *Cooking as Therapy*)

Introduction

The kitchen is where the action is! Think of all of the memories you've made in kitchens – the kitchen of your childhood home, your grandmother's kitchen, and your kitchen at the holidays. So it makes sense that we begin here. We want to spend some time getting this space in order, starting with the food and working our way out from there.

Remember, *the end game is not perfection*. In the kitchen, it's simple. You want to get your hands on what you need, when you need it, and spend less time on clean-up.

GIT

Fear Factor – Let's get it together! When it comes to cleaning out refrigerators, freezers, and pantries, in addition to getting rid of everything old and outdated, you also want to toss anything that makes you nervous or just plain scares you! Are you afraid to drink that milk? Does the thought of slapping that lunch meat on a sandwich give you visions of emergency rooms and long laborious bathroom visits? Then, get rid of it … even if the date indicates it's good.

Tupperware Test – Get rid of the unmatched, the distorted, and the hopelessly stained and smelly!

KIT

This week's Keep It Together tips focus on the little things you can do to make kitchen clean-up easier and to keep the kitchen from getting too far out of control in the first place.

Weekend Accelerators

There is a lot going on in the kitchen and there are a number of accelerators that would make great rainy day projects or possibly punishments for older kids! LOL!

The Weekend Accelerators for Week One range from computer work to assignments that require a lot of elbow grease. Some take just a few minutes while others could take a full afternoon. Remember, you don't have to do any of these but if you find something that seems doable … do it!

Extra

Beginning on Day 1 – make the commitment not to bring any new junk into your car. For 28 days, every time you get out of the car, take something with you. Throw away extra cups, fast food bags, old magazines and papers. When you arrive home in the evening, as you grab your purse and your bags, grab a pair of shoes, a kid's toy, something. When you get in the house, put it where it belongs (in the closet, in the dishwasher, in the toy chest in the kids' room).

Day 1: Refrigerator Run-Through

Throw out everything in the refrigerator that is outdated – cheeses, lunch meats, milk, and yogurts. Get rid of any fruits and vegetables that are moldy, hairy, furry, gooey or otherwise inedible. Check the refrigerator door and get rid of anything that you can't remember buying in the past year.

Bottom Line: If you're scared to cook with it or even open it, toss it. When in doubt, throw it out! If you can, salvage the containers.

Now, move to the freezer. What's the golden rule in this frozen wasteland? If you cannot recognize it, dump it. If the bag of vegetables is open and has been for several months, toss it.

If you question it – even a little bit – throw it away. If you are worried about 'wasting' food, consider this: You weren't going to eat it anyway! You are already wasting it and now it's wasting space in your refrigerator or freezer.

Put any salvaged containers in the sink; fill it with piping hot water and liquid dish detergent. If you have Tupperware that is retaining the smell of spoiled food, after cleaning it, soak it overnight in a combination of hot water and white vinegar.

Day 2: Cabinet Dive and Dump

Dive into the cabinets and the pantry and focus on the food. There could be more in your pantry than food but the focus today is on all things edible and nothing else.

You don't need to throw away unopened boxed foods and canned goods. Consider donating them to a shelter or food drive. If it's been opened and seems stale, or if you are reluctant to cook with it, toss it.

I realize that canned goods can almost last forever, so technically you can keep them forever. But if you have things that are not being eaten, ask yourself why you are keeping them. Are you pushing aside foods you have no intention of eating just to get to something you really need? Are you running out of space because so many miscellaneous items are in the way?

Make a mental note of the things you are discarding. Are these items you were going to use for a special recipe that never got made? Are these items that you or your family tried but don't really like? Did you buy it just because it was on sale? Consider what you aren't using and why you aren't using it as you prepare your shopping list.

Day 3: Sort and Separate

You've gotten rid of the excess in the pantry and cabinets. Take a few minutes to reorganize items. There are two ways you can organize. You can put like items together: soups, canned veggies, rice, pastas, cereals, baby food, and sauces. Or, you can place items that you use frequently together. In other words, if you make chili, place the chili beans and the canned diced tomatoes next to each other.

Next, turn the labels so they face forward and are easy to read. You don't have to go further than this ... *unless you want to*. If you feel the need to alphabetize, go for it! If not, remember, the assignment is to group like items together and that's it!

If you have several cans of the same item, instead of putting them one in front of the other, stack them on top of each other – vertically, if you can. This can save space and it makes it easier to see exactly what you have and how much.

If you have young kids, keep things they like and that you encourage them to eat (the legal treats) at their level, where it's easy for them to reach. Keep the other treats (cupcakes, cookies, chips...) a little higher up and out of their reach.

Day 4: Over and Under

Today you will tackle *two* different areas: the area under the kitchen sink and the space on top of the refrigerator. As you go under the sink, get rid of any empty products or items you have purchased and not used. Organize what remains: dishwasher detergents and Jet Dry together, air fresheners and disinfectant sprays together, glass cleaners together, sponges, etc...

Kitchen sponges are the number one source of germs in the kitchen. You want to change them often (every few weeks or at least once a month). You can also zap a used sponge in the microwave for 2 minutes. That's usually enough time to sanitize it and kill the germs. Just make sure the sponge doesn't have any metal in it. You can also throw your sponge in the dishwasher to sanitize it.

Next, grab a sturdy chair and go on an expedition. Exactly what is on top of that refrigerator? For some, it's a great space for snacks or cereals. Others use it to store wine and other beverages. Some use it to store plastic cups, and storage items. Others still use it as a catch-all, a second 'junk drawer.' Only you know what resides over your fridge and only you know what you want to do with that space.

As you approach this assignment, understand how you want to use your space. What exactly is it that you want to use this space for? Get rid of any random items and, of course, anything stale and out-dated.

If you run out of time for this assignment, make this a quick Weekend Accelerator!

> *Bottom line is, if you do not use it or need it, it is clutter, and it needs to go."*
> *~ Charrise Ward*

Day 5: Tupperware Test

Remember when you bought that Tupperware or those snazzy Rubbermaid canisters? Everything was so nice and pretty. Now? Not so much. You haven't seen the tops of several items in years. Others are so discolored and misshapen that, to be honest, you're reluctant to put anything in them. What about the one that still smells like salmon?

Today, you want to go through the plastic containers and get rid of lids that don't have canisters, canisters that don't have lids and anything that makes you go "Ewww."

> **Congratulations**! You've finished your first week of organization! You've gotten off to a great start; but you don't want to do all this work just to mess it up again. What follows are some easy tips you can implement now that you've gotten it together (GIT) so that you can keep it together (KIT).

Keeping It Together (KIT)

Drop Before You Shop! Do a quick version of the refrigerator run-through every time you prepare to grocery shop. Throw out tired leftovers and dump outdated or spoiled items.

Respect the System: When you return from the store don't just dump the new stuff into the cabinets – take a moment (and it only takes a moment) to put the soups with the soups, the pasta with the pastas, etc…

Use your dishwasher silverware caddy. Most dishwashers come with a silverware caddy that has sections. Get in the habit of putting all the large forks in one compartment, small forks in another and so on. If you don't have a dishwasher, a lot of dish drying racks have a similar set up. This makes it a breeze when it comes to putting these items away.
CAUTION: While it's nice to have your silverware nice and neatly nested and stacked in your drawer, you do not want to nestle or stack them in the silverware caddy. If they are nestled together in the dishwasher, they won't get clean.

Clean as you cook. Keep a sink full of hot soapy water when you start cooking. As you cook, take a minute to clean your pots and pans as soon as you're done with them.

Emergency! There are times when you will need to make a last minute meal or when your third grader informs you, at bedtime, that he needs to bring a treat to school in the morning. In times like these, it helps if you have something quick on hand. Make a list of all the emergency goods you will need to make that last minute meal or bake those last minute cookies or cupcakes. Shop for those items and make sure to keep them on hand.

Weekend Accelerators

Clean the refrigerator and the freezer: Remove everything and wipe down the surfaces. Clean out the fruit and vegetable bins. Consider lining the bins with paper towels so if that tomato or cucumber goes to mush, it will be easy to clean up.

Countertop Clearing: The prime piece of real estate in your kitchen is the countertop. Take an inventory of what is taking up that valuable space. If you don't use it on a regular basis, get it off the countertop (toasters, blenders, bread makers …). Store them in a cabinet or in the garage. Better yet, if it's something you rarely (or never) use, consider selling it on Craig's List or giving it to a friend who needs it and will use it.

Computer Time: If you are using a version of Microsoft Office, there are free grocery list templates in Excel. Usually located under the *New* option, you can find a link to Office Templates Online. Once you download your list, customize it to reflect the foods that you and your family eat. Print it and put it on the refrigerator. As you run out of items, check them off on the list. Now, when it's time to hit the store, you have your list and it's already done!

Kitchen Table: If yours is a repository for miscellaneous papers and other odds and ends, get rid of any papers and items you don't need. Keep the papers you need to keep in a pile (you'll be a step ahead during Week Four!).

Cook It: If you have found items in your pantry that you purchased for a special recipe – why not make it? You probably have most of the ingredients already. So prepare it!

Cork It: If the front of your refrigerator is filled with coupons, reminders, emergency phone lists and anything and everything else, consider purchasing a small cork board that can be placed on the *inside* of a pantry or cabinet door. Use that to post your coupons, reminders and phone list. Save the refrigerator for fun magnets and your children's works of art!

Useful Utensils: Go through your utensil drawer and get rid of any items you don't use or need. Then, take the items you use most often and place them in a container you can keep on your countertop where they are easy to get to.

Prep for Week Two

We've got a little more work to do in the kitchen before heading to the bathroom. So before Tuesday morning, take a look around and make sure you have a couple of baskets or boxes or bins for hair accessories, make-up, and other items you use in the bathroom. You probably have a few. If you don't, they are inexpensive and easy to find at Wal-Mart, Target, or Family Dollar. I got a great deal on some very colorful bins at Office Max once!

Week Two

"If I want to be alone, some place I can write, I can read, I can pray, I can cry, I can do whatever I want - I go to the bathroom."
~ Alicia Keys (Grammy Award-winning Singer)

Introduction

After one more day in the kitchen, we'll be moving to the bathroom. If you have more than one bathroom, start with the master bathroom or the one you use the most. Repeat the same exercises in the other bathrooms. Guest bathrooms should be pretty easy. If you have older kids, enlist them to help with their bathrooms. Have them place everything they're thinking about throwing out into a box so that you can review it first.

GIT

To Junk or Not to Junk? – Before we leave the kitchen we want to rummage through the junk drawer. Some of it you will want to keep, but – and let's be honest here – there is some junk that you can throw away. You probably don't need the keys to your freshmen dorm room anymore.

A Better Bath – It's a place of privacy. It can be a place of sanctuary. It's a place where we go when we are sick, where we perform our beauty rituals and where we share priceless moments with the children. It's also a place where we waste a lot of time and create a lot of clutter. Having a little order in the bathroom can speed up our morning rituals and that's always a good thing.

KIT

We want to get some processes in order that will keep the bathroom functional and fast. Plus, this week, we look at integrating some simple systems to keep from re-cluttering the bathroom.

Weekend Accelerators

Weekend Accelerators for Week Two include easy ways to add some organization to the bathroom, wading through your sea of old magazines and the prospect of re-gifting (but not the tacky way!).

Extra

Beginning on Day 8 – Take 5 minutes a day to begin deleting your emails. Most of the time your emails are arranged by date, but sifting through them chronologically can waste a lot of time! Briefly arrange them by From or Sender to get rid of multiple messages at once.

If you are using Outlook, Lotus Notes or another non-Internet-based email program, try this technique to delete multiple messages quickly. To select multiple messages at once, click on the first message, hold down the SHIFT key and click on the last message you want to delete. This will highlight the entire group of messages. Just hit DELETE and you will delete them all.

For example, you have your messages in order by *From*. Now all your *Joke of the Day* messages are grouped together. Click on the first one, and then scroll down. Find the last *Joke of the* Day message, and before you click on it, hold down the SHIFT Key. Now, click the last message. All the *Joke of the Day* messages should be highlighted. Press DELETE.

Holding down the CTRL key, while selecting messages, will allow you to select multiple messages that aren't necessarily next to each other. Let's say all the messages from your sister are together but you don't want to delete all of them. While holding down the CTRL key, click on the ones you want to delete. Once you have them selected, let go of the CTRL key and press DELETE.

If you are using Yahoo! or Hotmail or another Internet mail program, the CTRL and SHIFT tricks won't work. However, there is usually a check box on the header row that allows you to select all the items on that page. You can also use the check boxes in front of each message to select the messages you want to delete.

It might be easier to use the checkbox to check all of the messages on a page and just deselect the ones you do not want to delete.

Day 8: Junk or Bunk?

You have a junk drawer. I know you do. It's probably in the kitchen but it could be in the laundry room, your bedroom or even the garage. The great thing about a junk drawer is that it houses all sorts of unexpected treasures! However, it also contains a number of things that have outlived their usefulness: keys to your old workplace (the one you left five years ago), manuals for items you don't own anymore (like that old VCR or your cassette boom box), plus random stuff you don't need that just got stuck in the junk drawer because, well, it's the junk drawer.

The goal is simple: throw away the junk and free up some space. It's inevitable. You *will* get more junk. The question is, where will it go if the junk drawer is full?

A lot of times, you have *multiple* junk drawers throughout the house. Focus here on the worst one. The rest could make a great Weekend Accelerator project.

Day 9: Is It Good For You?

Go through the medicine cabinet and throw away any expired medicines. Throw out prescriptions you no longer need. If the dentist gave you painkillers last year when you had your root canal and you took a couple but have a few left, discard them. Do this in all of your bathrooms. *This is one assignment you should not delegate to the kids!*

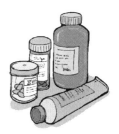

Studies have shown a number of medicines to be perfectly fine to take after the expiration date. However, certain medications like nitroglycerin (for heart ailments), insulin and liquid medications often degrade faster than others. Another factor is that most medicines should be stored in a 'cool, dry place' for best use. Most bathrooms are a little too humid for optimal storage conditions. If you are in doubt, call your local pharmacist.

Day 10: Toss the Gloss

This is going to hurt a little. Take a trash bag into your bathroom, then take a good, long, hard look at your shampoos, conditioners, make-up, skin care products and bath and shower gels. Take a deep breath and get rid of everything you don't currently use. [1]

---

[1] Nicole Carter, "Average Woman Will Spend About $13,000 on Makeup in Her Lifetime" [http://www.nydailynews.com/lifestyle/2010/03/10/2010-03-10_average_woman_will_spend_about_13000_on_makeup_in_her_lifetime_study.html#ixzz0IrZrIxty] March 10, 2010

- The shampoo you used once but it left your hair too dry ... *toss it.*
- The conditioner you used to use before you switched to the new conditioner you absolutely love ... *toss it.*
- The lipstick that looked amazing under the florescent lights of the department store but was too bright when you got it home ... *toss it. Unless you have a little girl who likes to place dress-up; she'd love to have some real grown-up lipsticks!*
- All the shower gels, bath salts and bubble baths you got for the holidays but hate the smell of ... *toss them.*
- All the stuff you bought just because it was on sale or because it was part of some 'free gift' promotion ... *toss them!*
- The hair scrunchies and clips you used before you got your haircut ... *toss them too!*

In some cases, you may have spent a lot of money on these products and might be reluctant to toss them. I want you to think about how much time you waste sifting through make-up you never wear. Think of how much space you are losing to bottles of product that you will never use.
NEWSFLASH: *If you aren't using it and you don't plan on using it, you are already wasting it.*

Day 11: All Together Now

Yesterday hurt a little. But now, you are looking at a space that is occupied by only the things you need, you like and you use. Your time today is spent putting those items together. You should have your make-up in a make-up case. You should have all of your hair accessories together, your combs and brushes together, shampoos and conditioners together, hair sprays and spritzers together. You probably have these containers; if you didn't, you should have gotten some inexpensive containers over the weekend.

Also take a moment and put all your cleaning supplies together. Consider putting items close to their function: toilet bowl cleaner – next to the toilet bowl; bath cleaner – next to the bath tub. Place everything else together underneath the sink or in the alternate storage space if you don't have an under sink area.

Imagine how nice it will feel tomorrow morning when you can come into your bathroom and put your hands on exactly what you need! Ah! The miracle of organization!

Day 12: The Same Thing All Over Again

Most homes and apartments have more than one bathroom, although the master bath tends to be the worst when it comes to organization. Today, take a stab at the other bathrooms. Get rid of the old medicines in the kid's bathroom, sort and organize all of their accessories and products as well. The guest bathroom should be a breeze.

What if you just have one bathroom? Well, take a look at some of the weekend accelerators and take a shot at one of those (you didn't think I'd give you a day off, did you?).

Congratulations! Two weeks down. When you start next week, you will be halfway through the program. Tell the truth; it hasn't been that bad, has it?

Keeping It Together (KIT)

- ✓ **Words of Wisdom**: My mother would tell me, as she looked at my messy adolescent bedroom, "Don't make a mess and you won't have a mess to clean up." Get in the habit of putting things away as you use them. Hang up your towel when you are done drying off. Put your dirty clothes in the hamper right away (more on this next week). Put the make-up back in your make-up bin as you use it.

- ✓ **Take It Back**: When it comes to cosmetics, if you get home and find the color doesn't look as good as it did at the store … while you still have the receipt, take it back. You can get your cash back or make another purchase. But don't keep something you don't like. It wastes space and money!

- ✓ **Keep It In the Car**: Yes, I know you promised not to put any new clutter into the car; however, there is an exception. If you have something like make-up, clothing or other items that you plan on returning, keep the product and the receipt in a bag in the car. This way, as you are out running errands, when you pass by Macy's, you can grab that sweater and receipt and return it. It beats making a separate trip!

- ✓ **Lose What You Don't Use**: When you find the new shampoo or skin care regime you love, get rid of the one you no longer use. Remember it's not wasteful to throw it away if you were never going to use it.

- ✓ **Take a Moment**: The next time you are looking for something in your junk drawer and you come across something you no longer need, take a second, right then, to toss it.

The name of the game is not creating new clutter.

Weekend Accelerators

Get Hooked: I promised that this program would not break the bank. And it won't. However, when it comes to the bathroom, your door and your walls offer some prime real estate. Get some cute and stylish adhesive hooks that can be used on the back of your bathroom door or along your walls. These can be great for storing towels, pajamas, blow dryers and even curling irons. Get your small kids hooked on hooks by placing them at a level that is accessible to them.

Magazine Mayhem: Admit it. You really don't have time to read through two years of Cosmopolitan … *and you never will*. Go through your magazines and throw away the ones you've been promising to read. If you had certain articles earmarked, rip them out, place them in a folder and throw away the rest. When you are headed to the doctor's office, the DMV or anywhere else where a wait is inevitable, grab a couple of articles and take them with you. If it hurts your heart to throw the magazines away, give them to your hair salon or to a senior citizens' home. Take them to work and leave them in the break room or reception area. Give them to a friend who wants to read them.

Mail Madness: One-third of the mail you receive is junk. Go through all of your mail. Keep the most recent bills and discard the rest. It's called junk mail for a reason. Toss it.

Book'em: Take a look through your book shelves, magazines, and CD and DVD racks. Take any books, CDs or DVDs you no longer want off your shelves. Find a local CD Warehouse or similar store where you can exchange your CDs and DVDs for cash or trade. You can donate the books to your local library.

Regifting: Okay, it's kind of crass - but done correctly, regifting can save a ton of time and money, especially if your holiday season is filled with lots of holiday parties and events where little, 'inexpensive' gifts are expected. Find an area and store *new* items that you may have received as gifts or just bought and never used in a box (with the name of the person who originally gave it to you on a Post-It). Just remember the cardinal rule of regifting – never regift to the person who gave you the gift or in the same social circles as the original gift giver.

Baskets and Bins: If you don't have them, consider purchasing some small shelves or plastic drawers for the bathroom to organize your toiletries. Shoe boxes and envelope boxes (like the big ones they have at work) can also be excellent bathroom organizers.

Prep for Week Three

You knew it was coming. First the kitchen, then the bathroom, next the bedroom! And the closets! Start thinking about where you want to donate or share old clothes. Think about sisters and cousins who are currently wearing one of your old sizes *and* who share your sense of style.

Consider giving some of your children's old toys and clothes to a charity or to a friend or family member who can use them.

Week Three

"When things don't work well in the bedroom, they don't work well in the living room either."
~Dr. William H. Masters (Renowned Researcher in Human Sexuality)

Introduction

You knew we were going to get here sooner or later. It's later. It's time to tackle the chaotic closet, the overstuffed nightstand, and the disorderly dresser. It's time to deal with all those someday clothes and stacks of shoes ... not to mention the stuff that still has tags on it! Your bedroom may never be the immaculate vision you see on TV, but it can be easier to navigate.

If you have teens or tweens, encourage them to work this week on their closets. This is a great exercise for the kids. The KITs at the end of the week will also help keep them organized and on top of things.

GIT

You spend a lot of time in your bedroom. Of course, most of that time you're sleeping (or – ahem). Nevertheless, your bedroom should be relaxing and conducive to sleeping and seduction, rest and relaxation. Again, immaculate organization is not the goal. Let's see if we can get to the point where you can walk into your bedroom without experiencing a sense of dread.

Keep It in the Closet – Or Not. Closet clutter wastes a lot of time. We are taking a merciless approach to clearing your closet. You know the rule: If you haven't worn it in a year, get rid of it.

Taking a Stand – You probably don't read five books at a time, so why are there five books on your nightstand?

The Dresser Depository –Getting some of the excess from on top of the dresser, and getting together some of the stuff in the dresser is the goal.

KIT

There are lots of things you can do to keep your bedroom organized and the best part is that all of them take less than a minute. I'm talking 60 seconds *or less*. These are great ideas for you and even better ideas for the spouse and the kids.

Weekend Accelerators

Weekend Accelerators for Week Three continue the work we've started during the week. If you need more time in your closet or dresser, you'll have it. You can also use this time to focus on kids' closets and other closets in the house.

Extra

 Beginning on Day 15 – Take a couple of minutes a day and clean out an area of your purse. Get rid of old receipts, post-it notes, grocery lists, expired coupons and random junk. Then each day, tackle a different section of your purse:

> *The average purse weights 7 pounds!*

Make-up bag – get rid of the make-up you don't wear regularly, you've run out of and any duplicates;

Wallet – take out any expired coupons, old credit cards (and cards you don't want to use), and some of those store discount cards for stores you never visit;

Zippered compartments – find an area to collect your business cards (outside of the purse), and get rid of any trash or things you don't need;

Everything else: Books, magazines, day planners, kids' stuff, and everything else that makes that bag so heavy to carry! [2]

---

[2] Guenn Peterson, "The Average Woman's Purse Weighs Seven Pounds" [http://www.acetj.com/features/stupidnews.php?feature_id=3576] April 23, 2009

Day 15: The Nightstand's Last Stand

The nightstand is the junk drawer of the bedroom! If you can't see the clock on your nightstand, you might have too much stuff on top. If you can't find your journal inside the nightstand, there's probably too much stuff in there too! Go through your nightstand and get rid of anything that you don't need to have right next to your bed.

Limit the items on your nightstand to things you might need to reach for immediately from your bed. Think about what you need to have right there. Personally, I need my clock and my phone. I also like to have whatever book I'm reading on top and my journal and a pen inside.

Day 16: The Closet Flash

Okay, we are over halfway through this program. You and I, together, have made some pretty major strides. Now, I need you to trust me. "But Karyn," you say with exasperation and a touch of fear, "You don't know what *my* closet is like. I can't make a dent in it in 15 minutes!" You are right ... to a point. I'm not in your closet; but I do know that you can make at least a dent, if not more, if you give me your full attention for those 15 Focused Minutes.[3]

For this quarter of an hour, your goal, your ONLY goal, is to get rid of everything that doesn't fit, you haven't worn, don't like, or still has a tag on it after a year. Don't worry about shoes and accessories ... yet. Grab several boxes or bags. Mark them as follows:

- ✓ **Charity**: Stuff you are going to give away.

- ✓ **Friends**: Things in sizes that don't fit you but match the size and style of a friend/sister.

- ✓ **Consignment**: If you have top-of-the-line clothes in good condition, consider giving them to a consignment store. If they sell, you can make a little cash!

If you are reluctant to get rid of your clothes, keep this in mind: when you get rid of the old, you make room for the new (and the better!).

You are just getting rid of stuff today. You are not organizing; you are simply getting rid of the things you don't wear.

---

[3] Nikki Willhite "You and Your Wardrobe" [http://www.allthingsfrugal.com/wardrobe.htm] March 11, 2002

There are two ways to look at clothes that are too small:

1. Toss Them: When you lose weight, you can get excited about buying new, smaller clothes.

 2. Hide Them: There is nothing more demoralizing than a closet full of clothes that don't fit. If you can't bear to part with them, still get them out of your closet. Put them in a separate box, closet or other location. As you drop the pounds, you can go shopping with your own clothes! Put them back in your closet as you lose weight and can fit them again.

Day 17: The Dresser Dash

 Tell the truth, you made a dent in the closet! Now, we want to do the same thing with your dresser drawers. Spend 15 Focused Minutes going through drawers and tossing bras that don't fit, old and frayed underwear, old faded t-shirts (you know you don't need 30 of them!) and holey socks. The same rules that applied to your closet, apply here. Your discarded items can also go into your charity/friend/consignment bins.

We are focused today on the stuff inside drawers; we can handle the top of the dresser on another day (like tomorrow).

Day 18: The Dresser Top

Take a look at everything on your dresser. This is another area that collects clutter. When you empty your pockets or remove your jewelry, it all ends up on the dresser. There is nothing wrong with that, you just need to be more systematic about it. Take a look at the dresser top and get rid of any trash. Put the rest of the things in their place, go through any papers on the dresser, throw out the junk and put the rest in a pile on your desk or near your files.

You probably fall into one of two camps. You either have lots and lots of neat little baskets and boxes to store your stuff or you don't have any little baskets and boxes at all. Somewhere, there is a happy medium. If you have a lot of boxes and baskets, ask yourself if you need all of them. Can you consolidate some of your boxes and baskets? If you don't have any boxes or baskets, would a couple of nice boxes help you get organized? You probably have a few things around the house you can use. If not, a quick trip to Wal-Mart, Target, Ross, Marshall's, or TJ Maxx can help. And it won't break the bank.

Think about the things you commonly look for when you get dressed in the morning. Designate a special basket, box or just a specific location for things like: watches, keys, or cell phones. Get in the habit of keeping those items in that space. One less thing to look for in the hectic morning rush!

Day 19: Shoes Blues (and Accessories too!)

Remember a couple days ago, I said, "Don't worry about the shoes." Today, we'll worry about the shoes, and the purses, and the accessories! Take a look at the statistics listed below. Frankly, I think most women (definitely every woman I know) have more than 19 pairs of shoes. However, we want to take an unflinching look at the shoes we never have worn, the shoes that hurt too much to wear and the ones we've only worn once. Go through your closet and take a cold hard look at your shoes. You know what to do. Add the shoes to your charity/friend/consignment bags or boxes.

Remember, getting rid of these shoes leaves more space for buying new shoes. Give the once-over to your purses and your accessories too! [4, 5]

- The average woman owns **19** pairs of shoes.
- **88%** of women wear shoes that are too small.
- **60%** of women regret at least one shoe purchase.
- Most women have worn **25%** of their shoes only once.
- Women spend **40 hours** and **30 minutes** shopping for shoes every year, over the course of **15** shoe shopping trips.

As you go through your shoes, keep any nice empty shoe and boot boxes. They make excellent dresser and closet organizers!

---

[4] Belinda Goldsmith, "Most women own 19 pairs of shoes -- some secretly" [http://www.reuters.com/article/idUSN0632859720070910] September 10, 2007

[5] Diana Vilibert, "Test your shoe smarts with our heel trivia quiz!" [http://www.marieclaire.com/fashion/trends/articles/heel-shoe-trivia-quiz] March, 2009

> **WOW**! I am proud of you! This was a tough week, the week you were probably dreading, but you made progress in your bedroom, with your closet and with your dresser. Those are no small feats! Your closet and your bedroom overall should feel a little more comfortable and a little more relaxed and that's the goal. We want your room to be a place where you can rest and relax.

Keeping It Together (KIT)

- ✓ **Disrobing Secret**: Get undressed standing in front of the hamper and put your dirty clothes in it as you take them off. The key is to put items where they belong as soon as you remove them (this goes for shoes too). Put them away immediately and you won't have to make time to put them away later.

- ✓ **Hanger Habit**: If you wear suits and dresses that can be worn more than once, when you get dressed in the morning, put the empty hangers on the back of the door, the edge of your bed, or on top of the hamper. If it's easy to get to the hangers at the end of the day, you are more likely to hang your clothes up and put them back in the closet as soon as you take them off.

- ✓ **Favorite Spaces and Places**: Find some places where you can *always* put your keys, your purse, your watch, your cell phone. We focused on the bedroom this week, but these areas don't have to be in the bedroom. These spaces should be organic and logical. Is there an area or a hook near your door where you can place your keys? Is there an area on your dresser where your watch should go? Share these spaces with others in your house and get in the habit of keeping items where they belong.

Weekend Accelerators

Get Back in That Closet: Hopefully, you have made a pretty impressive dent in your closet. I bet it's looking better than you thought it would. However, if you still have work to do, get back in there! Pick up where you left off.

Sort and Separate: Here's another closet project. You don't have to have everything lined up by color from lightest to darkest, but it can be a big time saver to put like items together: pants, skirts, dresses, blouses, sweaters, suits. If you want to color-code, go for it! If not, that's alright too!

Don't Forget the Kids: If you have young kids, you'll want to spend some time in their closets. With younger kids, think about keeping things within their reach. Use hooks to keep things accessible for them. Designate a space for items like book bags and where you can layout their clothes for the next day. Otherwise, apply the same steps to cleaning their closets and dressers that you applied to yours. *If your kids are older, hopefully they did their own closets during the week. Take a few minutes to inspect the final results and to make sure they aren't giving away things you want them to keep.* Also, let the kids have a say about what items they want to get rid of – from clothes, to toys and games to old school projects – their opinions count!

Linens and More: Go through your linen closet. Now is the time to discard any mismatched towels, frayed sheets and stuff you just don't want or need anymore.

Shoe Box Shuffle: I asked you to save those shoe boxes for a reason. Go through your closet and dresser and use the shoe boxes to organize things from socks to bras to underwear to belts and scarves and other accessories!

Prep for Week Four

We've made a lot of progress as we make our way to the final week of the program. We will spend some time in the living room and the work/office area. By now, you should be using some of the KITs and thinking about some easy ways to maintain the level of organization you already have.

Week Four

"A good home must be made, not bought."
— Joyce Maynard (Author and Syndicated Columnist)

Introduction

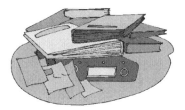

We've hit the major areas. Now it's time to handle the rest – living room and office. We want to deal with paper and excessive mail as well as the little things that clutter the common areas.

As we conclude, we really want to establish some good *Keep It Together* processes that will help you maintain the organization you've started. The key to keeping it together is consistency. If you develop a daily habit of hanging up your clothes or throwing them in the hamper when you take them off, then you don't have to make the time later to go back and pick them up!

Consistency and immediacy are critical to maintaining your new habits.

GIT

Remember progress, not perfection, is our goal and I'm sure you are making progress! We will develop special areas for things like toys, magazines, DVDs, and remote controls. I will also share with you a clear-cut, cheap and colorful way of organizing your most important papers.

There's No Place like Home – When it comes to the living room, a lot of the clutter actually belongs somewhere else. Jackets, blankets, shoes, toys and books all have 'homes'. Putting them where they belong is the first step to eliminating clutter in the common areas.

Table Top Tease – If you have a desk, is it covered in papers? What about your kitchen or dining room table? We need to go through those papers and find a system for controlling the critical paperwork while discarding the rest.

KIT

We will finish with a series of easy tasks you can do to keep things straight. Most will take less than a minute!

Weekend Accelerators

Our last set of accelerators will focus on some areas I've intentionally been avoiding: the garage and the patio. These sections take much more than 15 minutes to get a grasp on.

Day 22: Put It in Its Place

A lot of the clutter in your living room comes from things that belong somewhere else. So today's task is easy. Go through the house and put items back where they belong – books on bookshelves, shoes in closet, coats and jackets in coat closet, blankets and throws in the linen closet (or other location), glasses and plates in the kitchen, magazines in the magazine rack (or in a neat pile).

As you come across papers that you need to keep (pay stubs, bills, statements), put those aside in a pile. We will deal with them later in the week.

Toys present a particular challenge. If you have a chest or storage box, use it for small toys. However, you might have to think a little creatively for larger items that will not fit into a box. Consider having a specific section or area of a room (or the garage) for larger items.

Common areas are common because everyone uses them. Get everyone involved in keeping them straight. Make it into a game; give a special reward (picking what restaurant to go to, a reprieve from chores) to the person who does the best job keeping the area clean all week.

Find a location for all of your remote controls. A simple KIT is to put them all together at the end of the evening in the designated place or in a nice basket. Make it the last thing you do before you turn out the lights in that room.

Day 23: Mabel! Mabel! Get Those Papers Off the Table!

I haven't been to your home but I'm willing to bet that somewhere – kitchen, dining room, living room, den, bedroom, or desk – you have a stack of papers, maybe two, you've been meaning to go through. This assignment applies to that area (or those areas if there is more than one). I want you to spend 15 minutes going though the papers. Throw out what you don't need and, for the papers you need to keep, make four piles: papers you need to take action on, bills, items that need to be filed (statements, paystubs, recipes, etc.), and things you want to read. Consider a fifth file, if you have receipts and papers you need to keep separately for tax purposes.

> *The average American averages 560 pieces of junk mail a year!*

Go to any drug store, Wal-Mart, or Target. In the office area, you will find colorful two pocket folders. They usually cost less than a dollar. Get four of them in different colors. Label them: *Take Action*, *Bills*, *File* and *Read*. Place each of the piles in the appropriate file. Purchase a fifth file, if you need one for your tax-related paper and receipts. [6]

Day 24: Desk Is a Mess

Even if you don't have a desk, you probably have a table or computer station which functions as your de facto work area. This is the area we're working on today. Maybe you spent some time clearing the papers from this area yesterday. However, there are other items besides papers. Today we focus on organizing these. Chances are you have some organizers around your desk: a cup for pens, something for business cards, an organizer with various sections for paper clips, staples, post-its and so on. Spend some time today getting that area in order. Pens in the pen cup and so on. Straighten it out and put items where they belong.

 If you are keeping your children's art projects, drawings, report cards and so on, think about saving just a couple of items from each grade. If you aren't sure what to keep, ask your children which ones they like best.

Day 25: Filing Focus

Chances are, when you look at your pretty color-coded folders, the biggest and bulkiest one is marked *File*. Today is devoted to getting that file a little thinner. I'm assuming you already have files set up for your most common papers (pay stubs, insurance, bank statements, etc.). Place these papers into your existing file structure. I like to place things like pay stubs and bank statements with the oldest on the bottom and the newest on top. That way when you get a new one, you just put it in front of your existing files and they are already in order.

---

6 The Green Team, "General Recycling Facts" [http://www.thegreenteam.org/facts-tips.html]

Day 26: Lady's Choice

Today is your day! It's your choice! Spend your final 15 minute session wherever you see the need. Think your final 15 would be best spent in the kitchen? Go for it! If you could still use some work in the closet or in your dresser or with those shoes (all 19 pairs!), then that's what you should do. Maybe you still have some papers to file. That's cool too. This is your day; do whatever you want ... just make sure you do something!!! Maybe the kids' area could use a Power 15. Do it!

> **Yeah You**! Give yourself a hand. You did it! Even if you didn't do any of the accelerators, and you just spent 15 minutes a day, Monday through Friday, then you've spent 5 hours this month getting organized. Five hours seems like a snap when you do it in 15 minute increments! You should have less clutter, be more organized, and if you've used some of the KITs, you have some systems in place to stay that way. ☺

Keeping It Together (KIT)

- ✓ **The Circular File**: Open your mail while standing over the garbage can. Throw away all junk mail immediately. If you need the bill and the return envelope, keep those together and throw away the original envelope and all the filler. Take what's left and file it in your *Take Action, Bills, Read,* or *File* folder.

- ✓ **Use Your Filing System**: The mail you need to keep, the bills you need to review, the permission slips you need to sign, the invitations you need to RSVP, the articles you want to read (the ones you ripped out of the magazine that you threw away), all of these items have a home now. Use your colored folders to keep these papers organized. Always look in the *Take Action* folder first for things that need to be done. I make it a habit to check it once a week or more so nothing falls through the cracks. Skimming through it takes a few seconds. Things that need to be filed, paid or read have a place to go now, too. No more paper piles!

- ✓ **Do– Delegate– Move – Delete**: This is the mantra that will keep your email inbox clean. Handle your emails once. If you can respond quickly to an email, reply and delete the original. If someone else needs to handle it, forward it to them immediately and delete it. All junk mail in your inbox should be deleted immediately. If you need to keep certain messages, create folders and move them as soon as you've read the message. Every week or so, peruse your Sent Items and purge that folder as well.

- ✓ **I Spy**: If you are headed to another room or area of the house, look for any out-of-place items you can take with you. If you are watching TV in the living room and decide to call it a night, pick up your shoes and take them with you to the bedroom. Put them in the closet. If you are headed to the kitchen, pick up that glass and take it with you. Put it in the dishwasher.

Weekend Accelerators

Backtrack: Go back and complete any of the assignments you may have missed or that needed more time. Fifteen minutes can be a good start but some projects take longer. *There are a few areas that we didn't hit in this program, so this last set of accelerators is dedicated to those tricky areas.*

Garage: Garages range from sparse to so cluttered that a car can't fit into it (not even a Mini Cooper). Go through your garage. If it's stuffed, make a list of items you need and use in your garage and have your own scavenger hunt. Make sure to place those items where they are easy to find and access.

Laundry Room: Apply what you have learned in the program to this area. Get rid of items and products you aren't using. Put away any clothes or linens that tend to linger in that room. Put items in their place: irons, ironing boards, cleaning products, excess hangers.

And There You Have It!

Four weeks and a total of five hours spent getting it together. You have to admit, you have less clutter and more organization that you had when you began. Hopefully, you've picked up some tips along the way to help you stay organized. When you eliminate the need for perfection and embrace the need to be real, you start making progress.

The moral of the story is simple. You can do a lot with a little bit of time. Never underestimate the power of a Focused 15. Just 15 minutes here and there can help you in a variety of ways. 15 minutes can help you when it comes to cleaning the house, reading emails, returning phone calls and even writing that Great American Novel!

Get creative about how you want to use those little nuggets of time and you'll find that you can find the time for the things that matter most to you. Big strides come from small steps!

Extra Stuff

List of Tasks

Done	Task	Notes
	Day 1: Refrigerator Run-Through	
	Day 2: Cabinet Dive and Dump	
	Day 3: Sort and Separate	
	Day 4: Over and Under	
	Day 5: Tupperware Test	
	Weekend One	
	Day 8: Junk or Bunk?	
	Day 9: Is It Good For You?	
	Day 10: Toss the Gloss	
	Day 11: All Together Now	
	Day 12: The Same Thing All Over Again	
	Weekend Two	
	Day 15: The Nightstand's Last Stand	
	Day 16: The Closet Flash	
	Day 17: The Dresser Dash	
	Day 18: The Dresser Top	
	Day 19: Shoes Blues	
	Weekend Three	
	Day 22: Put It in Its Place	
	Day 23: Get Those Papers Off the Table!	
	Day 24: Desk Is a Mess	
	Day 25: Filing Focus	
	Day 26: Lady's Choice	
	Weekend Four	

Contract

I, _____, am committing to the ***Get It Together Girl Home Organization*** program. I agree to spend 15 Focused Minutes, Monday through Friday, over four weeks, completing the assigned tasks. I realize that weekends are optional; however, I agree to at least review the list of Weekend Accelerator projects for each week.

I also recognize that organization is not a one-time event but an on-going process. I will review the weekly Keep It Together (KIT) tips and implement the ones that will work best for me and/or my family.

I am committed to becoming more organized and effective and will discuss this program with those in my household and enlist their help, if possible.

_____   _____
Signature   Date

About Get It Together Girl Creator
Karyn L. Beach

Life Coach Karyn Beach is passionate about organization. More importantly, she is passionate about making life coaching and its benefits accessible to everyday people. Karyn is committed to empowering people and helping them develop the skills and the mindset they need to succeed. The name of her website and blog, *Lose the Excuses,* succinctly expresses Karyn's philosophy.

She says, "Don't have the time? You'll be surprised what you can do with the time you have. Don't have the money? It just means you have to be a little more creative. Don't have the motivation? Let's find out why and what you need to spark that internal flame."

The ***Get It Together Girl!*** series is one way that Karyn is reaching out to people and letting them know, "Yes, you can." Karyn says, "People dread getting organized because they think it takes big chunks of time and huge amounts of effort. Nothing could be further from the truth. You can achieve dramatic results with little nuggets of time."

Karyn has a Bachelor of Science in Journalism from Ohio University and her Core Certification in Life Coaching from Coach Inc. For more information on individual and group coaching or for information on coordinating a speaking engagement or workshop, visit Karyn online at **www.losetheexcusesnow.com**.

Cindy Canty
Graphic Designer/Photographer

Cindy P. Canty is the graphic designer and photographer responsible for the *Get It Together Girl* logos as well as all of Karyn's photographs. Cindy has a Bachelors of Fine Arts from Converse College. She specializes in wedding photography and portraiture. Samples of her work can be found online at **www.simplycreativecc.com**

Lose the Excuses

Visit Our Website
Lose the Excuses Life Coaching is about helping people overcome the obstacles that stand between them and the dreams and goals they want to achieve. Lose the Excuses offers a variety of products and programs that fit any budget.
Visit us at http://www.losetheexcusesnow.com.

Read Our Blog
Updated twice a week, the Lose the Excuses Blog (http://www.losetheexcuses.blogspot.com) is a unique mix of motivation and inspiration intended to move readers to take action! You'll find thought-provoking articles, inspirational videos and even delicious time-saving recipes.

Coaching Programs
Whether you want the intimacy of one-to-one coaching, the support of group coaching or the convenience of email coaching, we have something for you! Stop by and see what coaching programs are available.
http://www.losetheexcusesnow.com/coaching.html

Made in the USA
Lexington, KY
24 May 2012